HAL LEONARD HARMONICA METHOD BOOK 1

For C Diatonic Harmonica

BY LIL' REV

INTRODUCTION 2
HOLDING THE HARMONICA 3
READING HARMONICA MUSIC 4
   Notes 4
   Rests 4
   Staff ....
   Number/Arrow System ....
PLAYING SINGLE NOTES ....
   Lip Pursing ....
   C Major Scale ....
LET'S PLAY SOME TUNES 8
THE HIGH REGISTER 10
   Upper-Register Agility Exercise 10
MIDDLE TO HIGH REGISTER 11
   Partial Chords 12
SKILL BUILDING WITH FIDDLE TUNES 13
   Position Playing 13
   High-Register Melody 14
   Double Tonguing 15
RHYTHM AND ACCOMPANIMENT 17
UNDERSTANDING I-IV-V 18
BASIC 12-BAR BLUES 19
TONGUE TECHNIQUE 20
   Tongue Slap 20
   Kissing the Harmonica 20
RHYTHMIC AGILITY EXERCISES 21

HAND TREMOLO TECHNIQUE 22
   How to Do It 22
   Hand Tremolo Practice Tunes 22
   Playing Tremolo with Mutes 24
   Mute Showpiece 26
   Arpeggio Exercise 27
   ARP—2ND POSITION 28
   The Blues Scale 29
   No-Bend Cross-Harp Licks 30
   Boogie and Shuffle Blues Patterns 31
CROSS-HARP AGILITY EXERCISES 32
   Triplets 32
PLAYING OCTAVES 33
   Using Octaves in Blues 34
TEN TIPS FOR GREAT HARP TONE 36
BENDING NOTES 37
   Getting Started 37
   Holes 1–3 38
   Holes 4–6 40
   The Headshake 40
   Standard Blues Licks 41
   Two Bending Hacks 42
BENDING THE BLUES 43
   Songs with Bends 43
   Exercises and Songs 44
   Talking Harmonica 45
PLAYING IN MINOR KEYS—3RD POSITION 46
   Songs in Minor Keys 47

To access video visit:
www.halleonard.com/mylibrary

Enter Code
6718-1358-1707-0215

ISBN 978-1-54008-757-7

Visit Hal Leonard Online at
www.halleonard.com

Contact us:
Hal Leonard
7777 West Bluemound Road
Milwaukee, WI 53213
Email: info@halleonard.com

In Europe, contact:
Hal Leonard Europe Limited
42 Wigmore Street
Marylebone, London, W1U 2RN
Email: info@halleonardeurope.com

In Australia, contact:
Hal Leonard Australia Pty. Ltd.
4 Lentara Court
Cheltenham, Victoria, 3192 Australia
Email: info@halleonard.com.au

INTRODUCTION

Welcome to the *Hal Leonard Harmonica Method, Book 1*! The book that you're holding is much more than just another harp methodology. I'd like you to think of it as an open door to a living, breathing world of musical magic!

I was just 12 years old when I got my first harmonica in a junk drawer swap with a neighborhood pal. I traded some baseball cards for my first harmonica, and looking back, I'd like to think that I got the better end of the deal! It was way back then that I, like you, took my first step towards learning to play the harmonica. I could never have imagined the people, places, and things that I would discover as a result of my connection to the harmonica.

Now that you're ready to start puffing and blowing, dare I say that—given the right mixture of practice, patience, and persistence—learning to play the harmonica is going to change your life for the better... as in mo' better! Whether you're interested in playing blues, rock, folk, Celtic, classical, jazz, country, or pop, the humble harmonica can take you there.

I've often said that the harmonica is one of the easiest instruments to get started on. What this means is, if you practice 20 to 30 minutes a couple times a week, you'll continue to make gradual improvements in your ability to carry a tune, chord or "chug" along, play a riff, bend a note, or any number of cool effects that harmonica players like to employ.

The *Hal Leonard Harmonica Method* is your springboard into a world of music that's as welcoming as it is endless. This is just one stop along the way. Ultimately, it'll serve as the foundation for a lifetime of joyful music-making.

The harmonica has one of the most hauntingly beautiful and evocative sounds of any free-reed instrument. It is capable of expressing sadness in its bluesy trills, or it can be joyfully uplifting with its percussive punch. The full range of sound the mighty "pocket piano" can muster is nothing short of impressive. One thing is for certain, you'll always be able to make music wherever you wander—on the front porch, at an open mic, in front of a camera, at a gig, or at a jam—the harmonica will always be a welcome addition!

Musically,

Lil' Rev (*www.lilrev.com*)

ABOUT THE VIDEOS

To download or stream the accompanying video lessons, simply visit *www.halleonard.com/mylibrary* and enter the code from page 1 of this book. Video icons ▣ appear throughout the book to indicate the corresponding video lessons. Some icons are shown with a time code, allowing you to locate a specific example within a larger video lesson.

HOLDING THE HARMONICA ▶️

There are many ways to hold the harmonica. Variation is the result of what is most comfortable for each individual. I urge you to explore what makes the most sense to your body, while also learning from those who've gone before, in order to figure out what works best for you.

Here are three of the most common ways to hold your harmonica:

1.

One-Handed Style:

Sometimes, the use of just one single hand is both a comfortable and an acceptable way to play. Let the harmonica rest gently in between the thumb and index finger of your left hand, while your other fingers extend outwards to form a shelf. Think of holding a sandwich!

2.

Two-Handed Style:

The most common way to hold the harmonica is by using two hands to support the instrument. This is done by combining the one-handed style (see above; hold the harp in your left hand) with the use of your right hand. Once the harmonica is stable in the left hand, place your right thumb under the harmonica, while abutting your other fingers over the top of your left hand. You can wrap the fingers or leave them pointing up.

3.

Harp Rack Style:

Another very popular way to hold the harmonica is geared towards multi-instrumentalists, or those who might like to teach themselves how to play two instruments at once! Place the harmonica in your neck rack and then begin to play your other chosen instrument. Practice the accompaniment, as well as the melody, together.

READING HARMONICA MUSIC

There are two ways to read harmonica music. The first is called **standard music notation**. While this system requires time to learn, once mastered, it allows you to read and play any piece of music you want. This book will provide you with the necessary rudimentary knowledge of standard music notation to learn to play the harmonica.

The second way is known as the **number/arrow system** and is extremely easy to learn. The numbers relate to the numbered holes on your harmonica and the arrows designate up (↑) for **blow** (blowing or exhaling out) or down (↓) for **draw** (drawing, inhaling, or sucking in). While this system is not as precise as standard music notation, it's much easier to learn. And, since our objective is to get you playing harmonica quickly, this book will rely primarily on the number/arrow system.

NOTES

A musical **note** will indicate two things:

1. **Pitch:** How high or low the sound is that the note represents.

2. **Rhythmic Value:** How many beats the note is held or played.

Here are four kinds of notes:

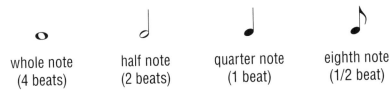

whole note	half note	quarter note	eighth note
(4 beats)	(2 beats)	(1 beat)	(1/2 beat)

Therefore, it follows that:

- Two half notes equal one whole note.
- Two quarter notes equal one half note.
- Four quarter notes equal one whole note.

RESTS

Just like notes, there are equivalent **rests** used in standard notation that tell you to stop playing for a certain number of beats. Rests are periods of silence between the notes.

Here are four kinds of rests:

whole rest	half rest	quarter rest	eighth rest
(4 beats)	(2 beats)	(1 beat)	(1/2 beat)

STAFF

A musical **staff** has five lines and four spaces. Each line and each space represent a different pitch.

A **treble clef** indicates the names of the lines and spaces by showing you where G is located, and for that reason it is also known as a G clef. Notice how the bottom of the clef curls around the second line. That line is the note G. The names of the lines and spaces are in alphabetical order going up, so the next space is A, the following line B, and so on.

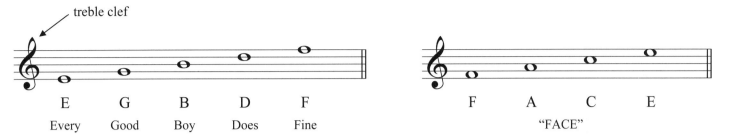

Measures

Notes on a staff are divided into **measures**. Measures help keep things organized so you know where you are while playing or singing a song.

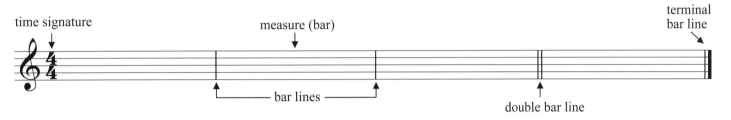

Time Signature

A **time signature** determines how many beats will appear in each measure. There are two numbers, and they are important. The top number tells you how many beats will be in each measure, and the bottom number tells you what type of note will equal one beat.

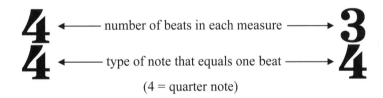

NUMBER/ARROW SYSTEM

Reading harmonica music with the number/arrow system is, as I mentioned earlier, very easy. If an arrow is pointing up (↑), it means to blow out. If an arrow is pointing down (↓), it means to draw in, or inhale. First, look at the number and find it on your harp. Then, look at the arrow and either draw or blow on that numbered hole. It's that simple. The downside is that, unlike the standard notation system, there is no indication of how long to hold a note. So, the number/arrow system is best used on old favorites and melodies that you already know. If you come across one you don't know in this book, watch the matching video a few times to get the idea.

REMEMBER: ↑ = blow   ↓ = draw

PLAYING SINGLE NOTES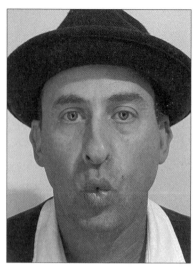

Lip Pursing Style

LIP PURSING

Once you're comfortable holding the harmonica, the next step is to learn how to purse your lips. To do this, you'll pucker your lips very small. It might be helpful to think of drinking through a straw, since that is the shape your mouth needs to make in order to form a small enough aperture, or hole, that can form a tight bond around any hole on the harp that you intend to play.

Now, take a close look at your harmonica. You should see that each hole has a number assigned to it, from hole 1 through 10. On each hole, you can blow as well as draw. To get started, let's explore the full range of the harmonica by trying to blow out and inhale in on a variety of different notes. First, try blowing into holes 1, 4, 7, and 10:

▶ 2:00

1↑   4↑   7↑   10↑

Were you able to hear the sound of one note at a time, or did it sound like a couple of notes bunched together? Go back and try this exercise a few more times; each time, try to purse your lips really small. If you are having trouble with this, then find a common drinking straw, put it up to your mouth, and practice forming a small aperture-like hole with your lips, á la puckering. Next, try drawing, or inhaling, through the same holes—1, 4, 7, and 10:

1↓   4↓   7↓   10↓

Did you notice how the holes in the lower and middle ranges (1 and 4) respond very easily to your breath, and the holes in the higher range (7 and 10) are much stiffer in their response? The more you practice, the more you'll get used to adjusting your breath to suit whatever hole you are playing; I like to think of this as compensating. Each hole has a corresponding reed inside. Each reed is a different length, thus requiring a different amount of breath.

Now let's try playing an ascending and descending major scale while thinking the corresponding solfège sounds to yourself as you play each note—Do, Re, Mi, Fa, Sol, La, Ti, Do...

Up the scale:

▶ 2:48

4↑   4↓   5↑   5↓   6↑   6↓   7↓   7↑

Now, down the scale:

7↑   7↓   6↓   6↑   5↓   5↑   4↓   4↑

C MAJOR SCALE

The C major scale is the foundation for most of what we'll be playing as you start out. In other words, if this were *The Karate Kid*, then practicing the major scale would be akin to "Wax on, wax off, grasshopper!" This scale will help you achieve your first goal of learning how to purse your lips and blow one note at a time. Speaking of notes, here's what the C major scale looks like, ascending and descending, when we add standard music notation. Each number has a note name on the staff. Notice that when a note goes above (or below) the staff, **ledger lines** are used so the notes are still easily identifiable.

C MAJOR SCALE
 0:20

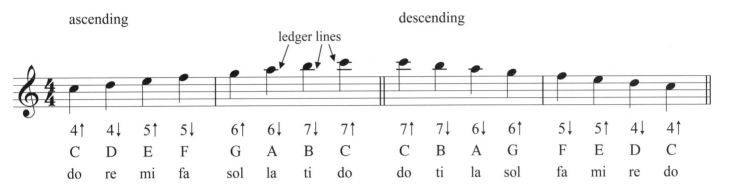

Play this every day until you feel confident that you can play the scale smoothly, articulating each note as you go from holes 4–7. Once you've accomplished this goal, it's time to move on. We'll continue to play all the notes in the scale, but let's break up the pattern a bit and zig-zag back and forth. This kind of pattern playing helps you build agility and familiarity with the notes in the scale.

ZIG-ZAG UP
 2:10

C	E	D	F	E	G	F	A	G	B	A	C	B	D	C
4↑	5↑	4↓	5↓	5↑	6↑	5↓	6↓	6↑	7↓	6↓	7↑	7↓	8↓	7↑

ZIG-ZAG DOWN

C	D	B	C	A	B	G	A	F	G	E	F	D	E	C
7↑	8↓	7↓	7↑	6↓	7↓	6↑	6↓	5↓	6↑	5↑	5↓	4↓	5↑	4↑

Excellent job so far! Now we'll try another pattern, called an **arpeggio**, that will help us continue to improve our single-note playing. An arpeggio is like playing a chord (which you'll learn more about later), except it's done one note at a time instead of all at once. My old mandolin teacher once referred to arpeggios as "broken chords," and I feel like that best describes them. Regardless, this exercise will help you improve.

4↑ 5↑ 6↑   4↓ 5↓ 6↓   5↑ 6↑ 7↓   5↓ 6↓ 7↑   6↑ 7↓ 8↓   6↓ 7↑ 8↑   7↓ 8↓ 9↓   7↑

LET'S PLAY SOME TUNES

Now that we've laid the foundation for playing single notes with the C major scale and some basic agility exercises, you're ready to begin playing some old, familiar melodies.

If your ultimate goal is to be able to play blues, rock, country, jazz, bluegrass, and pop music on the harmonica, then the following collection of old favorites will help you move in that direction. After 30 years of teaching harmonica, I know of no better way to improve than by attempting to play a lot of old, familiar melodies that we've all heard before. Doing so will hone your single-note playing skills, develop your breath control, perfect your lip pursing, and get you comfortable with holding the harmonica.

When you can play a couple dozen of these simple folk songs, you'll be ready to add many new techniques to your playing. Watch the video to ensure you've captured the right rhythm and phrasing. This will also train your ear for future endeavors when you might attempt to figure out how to play melodies without looking at a written score.

HOW DRY I AM!
▶ 0:23

3↑ 4↑ 4↓ 5↑   3↑ 4↑ 4↓ 5↑   5↑ 5↓ 5↑ 4↓   4↓ 5↑ 4↓ 4↑

GOODNIGHT LADIES
▶ 0:48

5↑ 4↑ 3↑ 4↑   5↑ 4↑ 4↓ 4↓   5↑ 4↑ 5↓ 5↓   5↓ 5↑ 5↑ 4↓ 4↓ 4↑

MICHAEL ROW YOUR BOAT ASHORE
▶ 1:17

4↑ 5↑ 6↑ 5↑ 6↑ 6↓ 6↑   5↑ 6↑ 6↓ 6↑   5↑ 6↑ 6↑ 5↑ 5↓ 5↑ 4↓   4↑ 4↓ 5↑ 4↓ 4↑

WILDWOOD FLOWER

5↑ 5↓ 6↑ 6↓ 7↑ 5↑   5↓ 5↑ 4↓ 5↑ 4↓ 4↑   5↑ 5↓ 6↑ 6↓ 7↑ 5↑   5↓ 5↑ 4↓ 5↑ 4↓ 4↑

6↑ 7↑ 8↑ 8↑ 8↓ 7↑ 6↑   6↓ 7↑ 6↓ 6↑   5↑ 5↓ 6↑ 6↑ 7↑ 5↑   5↑ 5↑ 4↓ 5↑ 4↓ 4↑

(HANG DOWN YOUR HEAD) TOM DOOLEY
▶ 1:43

6↑ 6↑ 6↑ 6↓ 7↑   8↑ 8↑   6↑ 6↑ 6↑ 6↓ 7↑ 8↓

6↑ 6↑ 6↑ 6↓ 7↑   8↓ 8↓   8↓ 8↓ 8↑ 7↑ 6↓ 7↑

WRECK OF THE OLD 97
▶ 2:10

6↑ 6↑ 5↑ 4↑   5↓ 5↓ 6↓ 7↑   6↓ 6↑ 6↑ 7↑ 7↑ 7↓

7↑ 7↑ 6↑ 5↑   5↓ 5↓ 6↓ 7↑   6↓ 6↑ 6↓ 6↑ 5↓   5↑ 5↓ 5↑ 4↓ 4↑

FRANKIE AND JOHNNY

4↑ 5↑ 6↑ 6↓ 6↑ 6↓   6↑ 5↑   4↑ 5↑ 6↑ 6↓ 6↑ 6↓ 6↑

7↑ 7↑ 7↓ 7↑ 7↑ 7↓ 7↑ 7↑ 7↑ 7↓   7↑ 7↑ 7↑ 7↓ 6↓ 6↑

5↑ 4↓ 5↑ 4↓ 5↑ 4↓   6↑ 6↑ 6↓ 6↑ 5↑ 4↑

CARELESS LOVE

5↑ 4↑ 3↓ 3↑ 3↓ 4↓ 4↑   5↑ 5↓ 6↑ 6↑ 6↓ 6↑ 4↓

5↑ 5↓ 6↑ 6↑ 6↓ 5↓ 4↑   4↑ 4↓ 5↑ 4↑ 3↓ 2↓ 3↓ 4↓ 4↑

9

THE HIGH REGISTER

The harmonica can be divided into three sections: lower, middle, and upper.

The middle register is great because it allows us to play a complete major scale without the use of **bends**. A bent or "flattened" pitch is accomplished through the use of controlled breathwork that allows the reed to vibrate at a higher velocity than normal drawing or blowing typically creates.

In the upper-register scale, from C to C, there is one missing note (B) which requires the use of a bend. We're not quite ready to tackle bending yet because we need to continue perfecting our single-note studies. However, the good news is that thousands of simple major scale folk songs can be played comfortably without the use of any bent notes.

It's important to make note of how each individual hole responds to a minimal amount of breath. You don't have to draw or blow too hard; just pucker your lips as small as possible and strive to play one hole at a time. Be patient, and with repetition, you'll improve!

UPPER-REGISTER AGILITY EXERCISE

This exercise is designed to give you ample opportunity to move around the upper register and familiarize yourself with how each numbered hole responds. Make sure to watch the video to hear how the rhythm of this exercise sounds.

ROUNDING THIRD
0:53

B	D	C	E		D	F	E	G		F	A	G	E		F	D	E	C
7↓	8↓	7↑	8↑		8↓	9↓	8↑	9↑		9↓	10↓	9↑	8↑		9↓	8↓	8↑	7↑

It's always good to know a patriotic tune.

YANKEE DOODLE DANDY

7↑ 7↑ 8↓ 8↑ 7↑ 8↑ 8↓ 6↑   7↑ 7↑ 8↓ 8↑ 7↑ 7↓   7↑ 7↑ 8↓ 8↑ 9↓ 8↑ 8↓ 7↑   7↓ 6↑ 6↓ 7↓ 7↑ 7↑

6↓ 7↓ 6↓ 6↑ 6↓ 7↓ 7↑   6↑ 6↓ 6↑ 5↓ 5↑ 6↑   6↓ 7↓ 6↓ 6↑ 6↓ 7↓ 7↑ 6↓   6↑ 7↑ 7↓ 8↓ 7↑ 7↑

Now let's try a holiday classic!

JOY TO THE WORLD
1:26

7↑ 7↓ 6↓ 6↑ 5↓ 5↑ 4↓ 4↑   6↑ 6↓ 6↓ 7↓ 7↓ 7↑   7↑ 7↑ 7↓ 6↓ 6↑ 6↑ 5↓ 5↑   7↑ 7↑ 7↓ 6↓ 6↑ 6↑ 5↓ 5↑

5↑ 5↑ 5↑ 5↑ 5↑ 5↓ 6↑   5↓ 5↑ 4↓ 4↑ 4↓ 5↑ 5↓   5↑ 4↓ 4↑ 7↑ 6↓ 6↑ 5↓ 5↑ 5↓ 5↑ 4↓ 4↑

MIDDLE TO HIGH REGISTER

"Straight harp" or **1st position** is the term harmonica players use when playing a song in the key to which the harmonica is tuned. In other words, a song in the key of C played on a C harmonica is being played in 1st position. Our studies thus far have focused on 1st position.

Typically, most of what you learn to play in the middle register can be played in the higher register as well. Let's look at a couple of tunes that illustrate this point. Harmonica players like to navigate all three registers because it lends some variety, or color, to an arrangement. Let's start with a middle-register version of the old-time ballad "Banks of the Ohio."

REPEATS

In the next song, you'll see a new music symbol called a **repeat sign** (𝄆) at the start of the song, and another one facing the other way at the end of the song. This tells you to repeat everything between the two repeat signs.

So, as you're playing through the song and you reach the second repeat sign, start back again at the top of the song—without pausing—and continue playing through the whole song again.

BANKS OF THE OHIO (Middle Register)

| 4↑ | 4↑ | 4↓ | 5↑ | | 5↑ | 5↓ | 5↑ | 4↓ | | 4↓ | 4↓ | 5↑ |

| 5↓ | | 6↑ | 6↑ | 5↓ | 5↑ | | 5↑ | 5↑ | 5↓ | 6↑ | | 6↑ | 6↑ | 6↓ | 6↑ |

| 5↓ | | 4↑ | 4↑ | 4↓ | 5↑ | | 5↑ | 5↓ | 5↑ | 4↓ | 4↑ |

Compare the arrangement above to this one in the higher register. It's the same tune and same arrangement of notes, minus the musical notation.

BANKS OF THE OHIO (High Register)

𝄆 7↑ 7↑ 8↓ 8↑   8↑ 9↓ 8↑ 8↓   8↓ 8↓ 8↑ 9↓

9↑ 9↑ 9↓ 8↑   8↑ 8↑ 9↓ 9↑   9↑ 9↑ 10↓ 9↑ 9↓

7↑ 7↑ 8↓ 8↑   8↑ 9↓ 8↑ 8↓ 7↑ 𝄇

PARTIAL CHORDS

We're going to continue looking at middle- and high-register melodies with "Railroad Bill," an old folk-blues favorite. It's often performed by fingerstyle and slide guitarists and is a great tune to play on the harmonica. In the first example, we'll explore "Railroad Bill" in the middle register, integrating **partial chords** or "double notes" (chord fragments or two-note chords) with the 5/6-hole blow, and then we'll follow up with a high-register variation of the same melody in tablature.

To begin, here's a simple exercise called "The Pea Vine Blues" to help you become familiar with playing double notes. The mouth organ can be incredibly vocal-like, thus, the vocalization of these syllables can help your mouth and tongue form the right shape. While playing this exercise, try to sound out the "da-da, ah-da" syllables. In addition to trying to shape the sound of the syllables, you'll need to *widen the aperture of your lips* so that enough air goes into two holes simultaneously, versus one at a time like we've been doing so far.

THE PEA VINE BLUES
 0:50

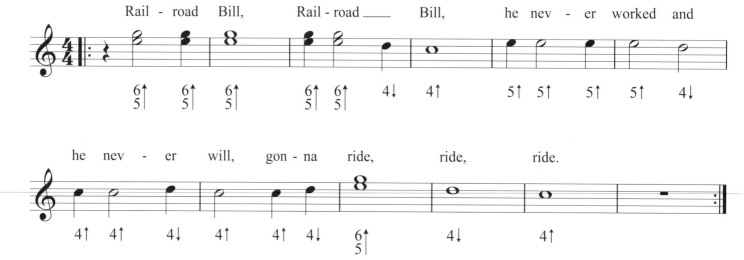

Now you're ready to play "Railroad Bill" in the middle register.

RAILROAD BILL (Middle Register)
1:08

Here's the higher version of the same song with single notes. Remember: lips small, like drinking through a straw!

RAILROAD BILL (High Register)
1:47

```
‖: 9↑  10↓ 9↑   9↑ 9↑ 9↓ 8↑   8↑ 8↑ 9↓ 8↑  8↓   7↑ 7↑ 8↓ 7↑   7↑ 8↓ 8↑  8↓  7↑ :‖
   Rail-road Bill,  Rail - road Bill,  he nev-er worked and   he nev-er will,  gon-na ride, ride, ride.
```

SKILL BUILDING WITH FIDDLE TUNES

"Old Joe Clark" is a perennial parking-lot-picker's favorite. It has become a chestnut in the canon of American music traditions, like bluegrass, old-time, and Western swing. Because this tune doesn't contain many notes, it tends to be one of the first fiddle tunes most people learn when they begin to build a body of instrumental music.

POSITION PLAYING

This arrangement is in 2nd position, which we'll study in depth later in the method. It is included here because it contains many of the same notes that we've been playing in our 1st position (straight harp) studies. For now, "wax on, wax off, grasshopper," and soon we'll dig into 2nd position.

First, let's compare the two positions:

1st Position	2nd Position (without bends)
4↑ 4↓ 5↑ 5↓ 6↑ 6↓ 7↓ 7↑	2↓ 3↓ 4↑ 4↓ 5↓ 6↑

CUT TIME

The fiddle tunes you'll be learning include a new time signature that you haven't seen yet called **cut time**, or 2/2. Cut time is counted as two beats per measure and the half note gets the beat. This is just like 4/4, but all the note values are cut in half. Since many fiddle tunes are played at a fast **tempo** (or speed), cut time helps keep the notation easier to read.

"Old Joe Clark" is the perfect tune for the harmonica because the breathwork required to play it includes a lot of in-and-out air movement. There are a lot of repeating single-note phrases, and this makes it a great choice for beginners.

OLD JOE CLARK

 1:06

*Throughout this book, music is sometimes notated down one octave for ease of reading.

HIGH-REGISTER MELODY

The siege of Boston began on April 19th, 1775. It lasted almost a full year as New England militia surrounded the town of Boston in order to prevent the British army from advancing by land. The militia came from all over the eastern seaboard, including Rhode Island. Nathanael Greene was the renowned general who led these men, and it was said that this melody was his favorite tune. More commonly, this melody is known in old-time dance circles as "On the Road to Boston." It is often played in the key of D and was originally a fife and drum tune that was played as the men marched.

There's nothing too tricky about this tune, though this arrangement is designed to give you a good workout in the upper register. Did you notice the repeat signs in the last tune "Old Joe Clark" and in the next song below? Play through the A section twice as indicated by the repeats; then, without pausing, continue on to the B section and play that twice through as well, ending the song on the last bar.

GENERAL GREEN'S MARCH

0:38

FIDDLE TUNES

Old-time fiddle tunes provide a wealth of skill-building challenges for the aspiring harmonica player, including agility, speed, breath control, single-note practice, multi-register movement, hand tremolo use, and note-placement familiarity. If you enjoy learning these types of tunes, there are many incredible players whose body of work can serve as a lifetime of inspiration, including Wailin' Wood, Glenn Weiser, Charlie McCoy, Mike Stevens, David Rice, Pegram and Parham, Mark Graham, and Brendan Power.

Folklorists have debated, for over 100 years now, whether the fiddle tune "Cripple Creek" comes from Cripple Creek, Virginia or Cripple Creek, Colorado. What's undeniable is that it's one of the top 10 most played fiddle tunes. Often sung, the refrain goes:

"Going up Cripple Creek, going on a run. Going up Cripple Creek, to have my fun!"

DOUBLE TONGUING

The ability to play repeating notes in rapid-fire succession requires the use of the **double-tonguing** technique each time you play fast eighth-note phrases, like those found in "Cripple Creek." Double tonguing happens when you learn to cut off the breath by touching your tongue to the roof of your mouth.

Say "doo da-da," and you'll notice that your tongue moves upward and slaps the roof of your mouth. Likewise, you can also say "tu-tu-tu-tu," to create a similar tongue movement. Here's an exercise using double tonguing to help you build these skills.

0:30

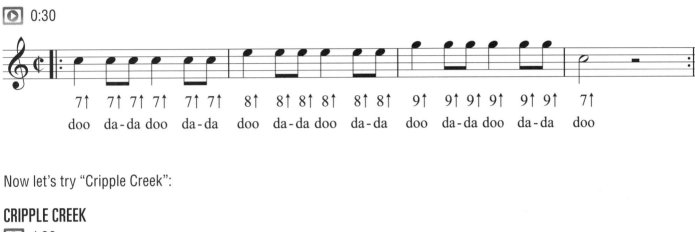

Now let's try "Cripple Creek":

CRIPPLE CREEK
1:30

"Angeline the Baker" is a banjo classic from the 1850s written by Stephen Foster, America's first popular songwriter. It's a catchy little tune that seems to linger long after it's played.

DOTTED NOTES

There's a new type of note appearing in the first measure of the B section called a **dotted note**. The dot next to the C notehead adds half the value of the note to itself. In this case, it's a **dotted quarter note**, so the dot adds half the value of the quarter note to itself. In other words, if a quarter note is usually one beat, then a dot adds a half beat to that value, resulting in one-and-a-half beats total.

ANGELINE THE BAKER

RHYTHM AND ACCOMPANIMENT

The harmonica is primarily thought of as a melody instrument, yet its rhythmic potential is otherworldly in breadth and scope. With a little practice, chord playing can be highly percussive and incredibly expressive in its own right.

Every harp player should learn how to be effective, not only when improvising and playing melodically, but also while accompanying other musicians. In the following pages, we'll explore a variety of techniques and concepts to help you become proficient at rhythmic-style accompaniment, or "backup." It's with this goal in mind that you'll be able to stay in the background when playing with other musicians, as your fellow jammers take turns playing the lead.

"Boil Them Cabbage Down" is a classic fiddle tune and certainly one of the easiest melodies to learn! First, play this simple melody in 1st position after watching the video.

BOIL THEM CABBAGE DOWN (Melody)
▶ 0:50

5↑ 5↑ 5↑ 5↑   5↓ 5↓   5↑ 5↑ 5↑ 5↑   4↓ 4↓   5↑ 5↑ 5↑ 5↑   5↓ 5↓ 5↓ 5↓   5↑ 5↑ 4↓ 4↓   4↑

Now, here's a 1st-position-style chord accompaniment. Remember, you'll need to open your mouth wider in order to play more holes at once. The chords we're playing here are C, F, and G—the I, IV, and V chords—which you'll learn more about on the next page.

BOIL THEM CABBAGE DOWN (Backup)
▶ 1:30

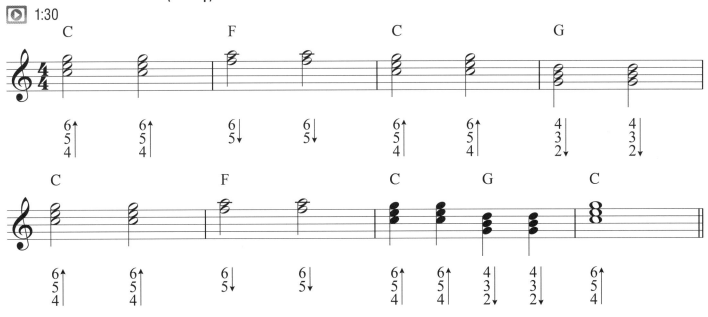

The next example is similar to the one above, except we'll play quarter-note rhythms rather than half notes. We'll also be in the key of G (2nd position) instead of C.

FOUR-BEATS-PER-MEASURE EXERCISE
▶ 2:29

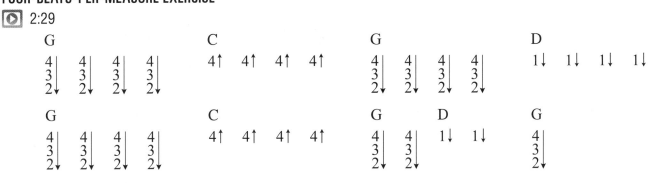

UNDERSTANDING I-IV-V

Most songs from folk, blues, country, or rock styles are based on the "1-4-5" chord progression. What's that, you ask? One (represented by Roman numeral I) is the key the song is in, and usually the first chord you would play. Let's say we're in the key of G, for example. The I chord is G. Four (IV) is the next chord, or four steps up from the G (G-A-B-**C**); in this case, four steps up from G would be C. Lastly, the five (V) chord is found by counting five steps up from G (G-A-B-C-**D**), so this would be D. Therefore, the I-IV-V chords in the key of G are G-C-D.

Below is a handy I-IV-V chord chart. It's good to memorize which chords go together in their respective keys. Then, as you become more comfortable with 1st- and 2nd-position chord work, your ear will improve upon hearing chord changes like those found in common song forms. Likewise, as your harmonica skills advance, you'll eventually gain the knowledge and understanding that it takes to play rhythmically and melodically in most of the common keys.

KEY	CHORD		
	I	IV	V
C	C	F	G
D	D	G	A
E	E	A	B
F	F	B♭	C
G	G	C	D
A	A	D	E
B	B	E	F#

Here's another way to look at it: take any major scale—for now, let's say the key of C—then assign each note in the scale a sequential number, or **scale degree**. I-IV-V will make a lot more sense when you see it this way:

Chords:	I			IV	V			
Scale Degrees:	**1**	2	3	**4**	**5**	6	7	8
C Major Scale:	**C**	D	E	**F**	**G**	A	B	C

Above, you can see that if we assign each note a scale degree, the notes in the scale also represent and correspond to the chord names that we'd use when playing accompaniment style on the harmonica. This is the kind of super useful information every musician should know!

RHYTHMIC HARP

Rhythmic harp at its finest? Listen to the work of the late blues harp icon Sonny Terry to hear how he punctuates his playing with rich chords, pops, smacks, hand tremolo, drum-like tongue slaps, octave jumps, and much more. Likewise, listen to Freeman Stowers' "Railroad Blues," DeFord Bailey's "Davidson County Blues," or even Salty Holmes' "Mama Blues" to hear other iconic pieces that showcase the rhythmic potential of the harmonica.

BASIC 12-BAR BLUES ▶️

The **12-bar blues** is the single most important chord progression that you can learn as a harmonica player. It is the bedrock upon which Chicago blues and roots rock rest. Practicing this progression will reinforce your ability to play accompaniment in 2nd position.

A 12-bar blues progression is made up of 12 four-beat measures, or bars. This progression repeats itself many times over the course of a song, from start to finish. Let's try playing the 12-bar blues example below.

To start, play each chord once per measure and sustain it for the duration of a whole note, counting "1, 2, 3, 4" to yourself. This will allow your ear to hear each chord played in a very basic way, without having to focus too much on what's going to happen next.

Once you feel confident with this, go back and play each chord four times per measure, as quarter notes. The slashes in the notation staff tell the player to choose a rhythm accompaniment style of their liking—in this case, basic whole notes and quarter notes.

12-BAR BLUES PROGRESSION

▶️ 1:28

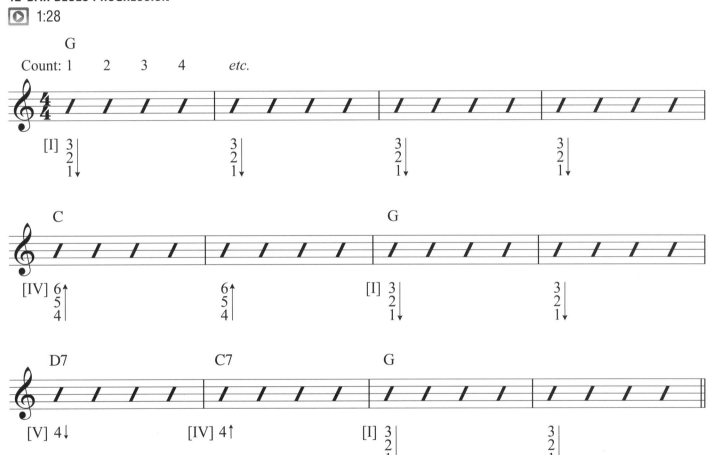

12-BAR BLUES HARP SONGS

To hear this progression in action, listen to "Hound Dog" by Elvis Presley, "Whole Lotta Shakin' Goin' On" by Jerry Lee Lewis, "Big Walter's Boogie" by Big Walter Horton, "Call Me the Breeze" by Lynyrd Skynyrd, "Move It on Over" by Hank Williams, "Before You Accuse Me" by Eric Clapton, and "Juke" by Little Walter.

TONGUE TECHNIQUE

TONGUE SLAP

One of the many harmonica techniques initiated by the tongue is a **tongue slap**. The tongue slap happens when the tongue moves up and down in the mouth and slaps both the roof of the mouth, as well as the soft palate. If you say the words "ticky-tocky" while breathing in on holes 1-2-3, you'll notice that your tongue is forced to move in an up-and-down motion. This motion creates a percussive train-like effect that can be integrated into literally any song or style that you choose. This can be done on the inhale as well as the exhale breath, as long as you keep trying to say "ticky-tocky." It's one of many neat percussive sounds that you can coax out of the harp with the help of the tongue's natural movement.

This technique can be really effective when accompanying bluegrass, country, old time, rock, and blues styles. Make the exercise below a normal part of your practice routine and you'll reap great rewards later when you've got the funkiest, most rhythmic playing in the neighborhood! Remember to keep thinking and literally trying to say the words "ticky-tocky" as you play each chord.

THE TICKY-TOCKY 9-BAR BLUES

2:25

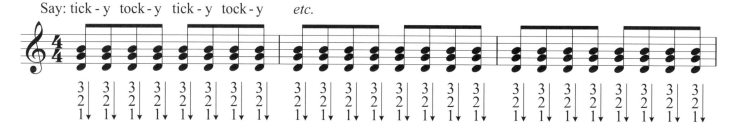

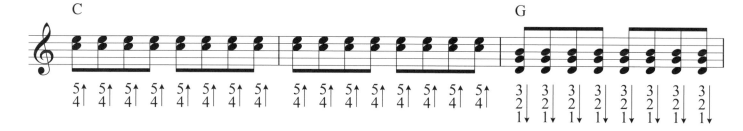

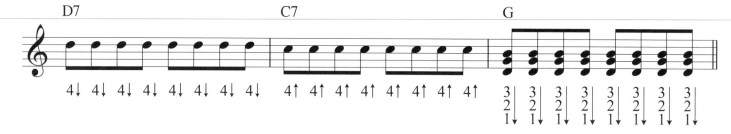

To compliment this lesson, watch the performance of my tune "Ode to Sonny" on the video. Listen for the "ticky-tocky" sound, as well as other percussive effects like "kissing the harmonica" (detailed below).

2:48

KISSING THE HARMONICA

Try drawing in on hole 2, but as you do it, "kiss" the 2-hole draw. It will create a smacking, percussive sound that the late Sonny Terry used to add to his fabulous playing whenever he was backing his partner of over 40 years, Brownie McGhee. Now, go back and play the 12-bar blues progression on the previous page. As you do, try to add a few "ticky-tocky's" and an occasional "kiss" to your accompaniment!

RHYTHMIC AGILITY EXERCISES

The following 8-bar exercise will give you ample practice changing chords at the start of each measure using a I-IV-V chord progression often called an **8-bar blues**. This type of chord progression is common in blues, rock, and country. It's also the same chord progression that's used to accompany "The Wreck of the Old 97" melody from earlier in the book (though it's in the key of C).

8 OF 97 CHORD EXERCISE

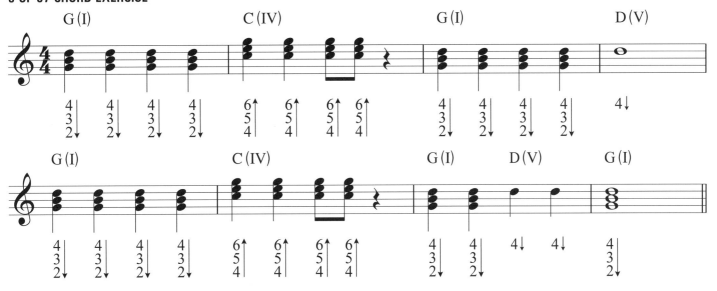

"The Stillhouse Trestle Blues" is fun to play and stands as a cool chord pattern from the Sonny Terry school of blues harp.

TRIPLETS

The next example includes a new type of note called the **triplet**. If you divide a quarter note into two equal halves, you get two eighth notes—counted as "1 and." If you divide a quarter note into *three* equal parts, you get a triplet, which are counted as "1 and ah." Sometimes it helps to count triplets with syllables instead of numbers, such as "tri-puh-let, tri-puh-let."

THE STILLHOUSE TRESTLE BLUES

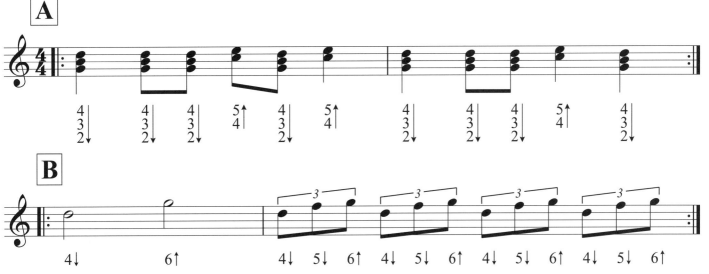

HAND TREMOLO TECHNIQUE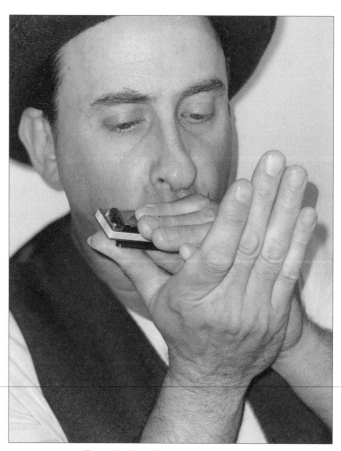

I often refer to **hand tremolo** as the "heart and soul" of the harmonica's unique sound. If you've ever watched a good harmonica player, it's usually only a matter of time before you'll see he or she waving their hand in front of the harmonica, either pivoting from the wrist (close in) or from a little further out, à la the blues approach. In the next couple of pages, you'll learn what tremolo is, as well as what it isn't. We'll explore how to integrate tremolo into your playing, when to use it, and which type of tremolo technique is best suited for which style of music.

To begin, let's discuss what tremolo is. **Tremolo**, at its most basic, can be thought of as an *intermittent change in volume*. When we wave our hand back and forth in front of the harmonica, it interrupts the sound, via a dampening effect. This wavering-like effect is often referred to as "the campfire sound," and is synonymous with the mouth organ. There are many ways to create that tremolo sound using your hands, as well as with implements like tin cans, glass bottles, PVC pipes, and mutes (more on this later).

HOW TO DO IT

1. Hold your harmonica with your left hand—fingers level on top and thumb securing the bottom.

2. Begin to play a note or melody.

3. Move your right hand back and forth in a fanning-like motion towards the harmonica. Pivot close in, from the wrist. This back-and-forth motion will create a tremolo sound.

4. Experiment with moving your right hand back and forth at different speeds; try fanning both fast and slow in order to hear the beats, or the "wah-ah-ah-ah-ah-ah" sound, at varying tempos.

Some songs, like "Home on the Range," "Shenandoah," and "Michael Row Your Boat Ashore," for example, sound better when the rate or speed at which you're moving your hand is a slower, rather than a faster, pulse. Do a lot of experimentation so you can figure out just how fast your hand should be vacillating back and forth.

I recommend that you first work on perfecting the "close-in" style tremolo; then later, when you become more advanced, you can begin to explore hand tremolo in which the hand fans from much farther out (fanning in towards the harmonica but starting 6–8 inches away from the wrist), as in the blues tradition.

Tremolo that Pivots from the Wrist

HAND TREMOLO PRACTICE TUNES

Here are some easy songs to begin with as you start trying to perfect the tremolo technique on the harmonica. Try to listen for the *long notes* in a melody, or rather, the places where tremolo will work well due to a note being held or sustained (half notes and whole notes). Fast songs with lots of notes, like fiddle tunes for example, typically don't sound good with hand tremolo.

SKIP TO MY LOU
2:47

5↑ 4↑ 5↑ 5↑ 5↑ 6↑   4↓ 3↓ 4↓ 4↓ 4↓ 5↓   5↑ 4↑ 5↑ 5↑ 5↑ 6↑   4↓ 5↑ 5↓ 5↑ 4↓ 4↑ 4↑

"Red River Valley" is an old cowboy favorite that works great with tremolo technique. If you are unfamiliar with this great melody, watch the video a few times. Remember to watch out for the half notes and tied whole notes—these long notes are a good place to use hand tremolo.

TIES

The next tune includes a music symbol called a **tie**—the long, curved line that connects different notes. A tie *ties* together two or more notes, resulting in a longer combined duration. For instance, a half note (two beats) tied to a whole note (four beats) would last for a total of six beats. Only the first note is sounded initially, then held for the full duration.

RED RIVER VALLEY

 3:10

3↑ 4↑ 5↑ 5↑ 5↑ 5↑ 4↓ 5↑ 4↓ 4↑ 3↑ 4↑

5↑ 4↑ 5↑ 6↑ 5↓ 5↑ 4↓ 6↑ 5↓ 5↑ 5↑ 4↓ 4↑ 4↓ 5↑

6↑ 5↓ 6↓ 6↓ 6↑ 7↓ 7↑ 8↓ 8↑ 8↓ 7↑

"Down in the Valley" is an Appalachian classic played in 3/4 time, which is often referred to as "waltz time." Count three beats per measure instead of four: "1-2-3, 1-2-3." This tune has some held notes that are great for tremolo practice. Remember to pivot from the wrist and waver your hand towards the harmonica slowly.

DOWN IN THE VALLEY

Down in the val-ley,
3↑ 4↑ 4↓ 5↑ 4↑

the val-ley so low.
5↑ 5↑ 4↓ 4↑ 4↓

Hang your head o-ver,
3↑ 3↓ 4↓ 5↓ 4↓

hear the wind blow.
3↓ 4↑ 4↓ 4↑

Hear the wind blow, dear,
3↑ 4↑ 4↓ 5↑ 4↑

hear the wind blow.
5↑ 4↓ 4↑ 4↓

Hang your head o-ver,
3↑ 3↓ 4↓ 5↓ 4↓

hear the wind blow.
3↓ 4↑ 4↓ 4↑

TREMOLO-STYLE HARMONICAS

If you enjoy the sound that is created by using the tremolo technique, many of the biggest harmonica manufacturers make tremolo-style harmonicas that are longer in length and can recreate the tremolo sound simply by drawing and blowing. Hohner's Echo, East Top's Professional Tremolo, and Suzuki's Humming Tremolo are all great examples.

PLAYING TREMOLO WITH MUTES

While most people learn to play the harmonica without doing much more than basic hand tremolo, common household items like hurricane lamp shades, tomato paste cans, broken bottles, PVC pipe, flexible plumbing joints, and many other open-ended implements have been used by harmonica players for decades to delay, reverberate, wah-wah, and distort the natural tone of the harmonica.

Early recorded harmonica history provides us with some clues as to how harmonica players created the unique sound, waxed onto old 78 records. Players like Deford Bailey, of early Grand Ole Opry fame, often played through a bullhorn to change the tone. Salty Holmes would often use glass bottles to create a wavering effect, and the Carver Boys used tin cans to mute the sound of the harp.

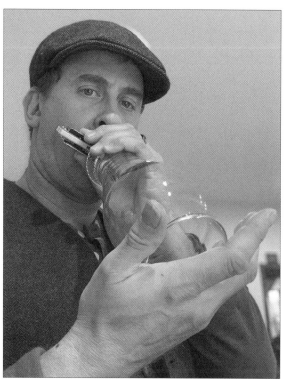

Hurricane Lamp Shade
 2:05

The hurricane lamp shade creates a deep resonant chamber in which a melody can dance around. It's by far one of the coolest mutes you can use. These come in many different sizes, though I recommend a medium-sized shade. Hardware stores and antique malls are a good place to find one.

Place the harp in your left hand while cupping the narrowest end of the shade with the open end of the harp abutting it; then, use your right hand to plunger-mute the wider end of the shade. The real secret to the harmonica sounding good with a hurricane lamp shade is to use a low-tuned harp like a Hohner Marine Band Thunderbird. Watch the video to see and hear this mute in action with the tune "Cluck Old Hen" played on a low G harmonica.

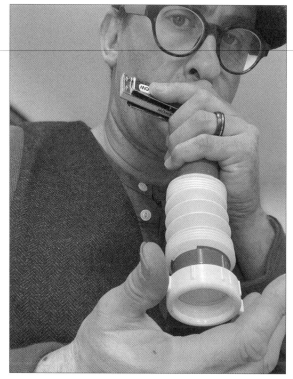

Flexible Plumbing Joints
3:44

You'd never expect to find a harmonica player in the plumbing section of your local hardware store, would you? In fact, the wide variety of plumbing PVC pipes and joints can provide an endless treasure trove of muted sound variety for the harpist!

Playing this type of mute is done the same way as the hurricane lamp shade. Place the harp in your left hand and grip the narrow end of the flexible plumbing joint; then, use your right hand as a plunger mute on the wider end of the pipe. The sound produced is mellow and sweet. It works well with regular-tuned harps as well as low-tuned harps. Watch the video for my rendition of "John Henry" played on an A harmonica with a flexible plumbing joint.

Tin Can

 5:31

Tin can mutes work best in the 6-ounce tomato paste variety. To find one, go to your grocery store and search for a 6-ounce Contadina Roma Paste can. Once it is emptied of its contents, cut the bottom off the can with a can opener. These are by far the most common type of mutes. The tone they produce is crisper, shrill, and with a lot less bass than the flexible plumbing joints and hurricane lamp shades. These are also much more comfortable in the hand than other mutes and much easier to manipulate. They are held the same way as the other mutes. The video demonstrates this with the song "Raincrow Bill" played on an A harmonica.

Photo courtesy of Alan Friedman

Commercial Mute

5:56

While I prefer tin can mutes, if you're looking for something a tad sleeker than a homemade mute, there's a hand-held, professional-grade harp wah/mute on the market called the Roly Platt Harp Wah. These sell for around $70 and are made of anodized aluminum steel. They have received high praise from several of my professional harp-playing friends, as well as myself! There are two models; I prefer the one with the finger latch as it's much easier to hold onto. Check out the video to see a demonstration of this mute with the song "Cajun Waltz" on a B harmonica.

Roly Platt Harp Wah/Mute

MUTE SHOWPIECE

The next piece can be played with hand tremolo but is included here because it's an extremely versatile tune that sounds really sweet when played with all kinds of mutes. "Beautiful Dreamer" was written by Stephen Foster and published after his passing in 1864. To date, it has been recorded by everyone from Bing Crosby to Ray Price, Marty Robbins, Jim Reeves, Roy Orbison, and Jerry Lee Lewis… to name a few. Remember, the best place to apply tremolo is anywhere you see longer, sustained notes such as half notes, dotted half notes, whole notes, or tied notes.

BEAUTIFUL DREAMER (Lil' Rev Adaptation)

ARPEGGIO EXERCISE

We'll finish our tremolo studies with a simple arpeggio exercise. Practicing arpeggios can help teach the tongue to direct the short bursts, or streams, of air required to play fiddle tunes, horn riffs, and classical pieces. First, play this straight with no tremolo; then, try adding your right-hand tremolo, pivoting from the wrist. Say "do-do, do-do, do-do, do-do" as you play each two-note phrase.

4↑ 5↑ 6↑ 5↑ 4↓ 5↓ 6↓ 5↓   4↑ 5↑ 6↑ 5↑ 4↓ 5↓ 6↓ 5↓   4↑

Lil' Rev teaching and performing at Sam Ash in Clearwater, FL (2014)
Photo used with permission from Chyrisse Tabone/Rock At Night

CROSS HARP—2ND POSITION

"Cross harp" is often referred to as **2nd position** among harmonica enthusiasts. It is the main position that you'll need to master if you want to play gritty, gut-bucket blues, rock 'n' roll, jazz, and country. Second position consists of mostly draw notes on the low end of the harmonica.

To play cross harp, you'll need to learn how to **bend**, or flatten, a pitch. Learning to bend notes will take some time, patience, and plenty of practice, but like thousands of others, one day you'll be playing blues harp!

The **blues scale** forms the basis for this position and allows for a C harmonica to be played in G. The best way to remember how this works is to establish the root or home key of a song, and then count up four steps.

1. Establish the key of the song.

2. Count up four steps to find what harp you'll need to play to be in that key while using 2nd position.

This begs the question: how many harps does any one player need? My answer would be: how many keys would you like to be able to play in?

Key of Song	Key of Harp Played in 2nd Position
G	C
E♭	A♭
E	A
F	B♭
F#	B
A♭	D♭
A	D
B♭	E♭
B	E
C	F
C#	F#

					1	**2**	**3**	**4**
	1	**2**	**3**	**4**	**5**	**6**	**7**	**8**
Here's a C scale:	**C**	**D**	**E**	**F**	**G**	**A**	**B**	**C**

Notice that if you count from G to C in the scale, it is four steps. This represents the process of how you can count up from the song's key and arrive at the right harp to play in 2nd position.

THE BLUES SCALE

If you draw in on the 2-hole of a C harmonica, you'll discover it's a G note, which is the root tone of the G blues scale: **G**-B♭-C-D♭-D-F-**G**. Here's the full blues scale with the flatted 3rd degree (B♭) and the flatted 5th degree (D♭). Watch the video a few times to get the sound of this scale in your ear.

G BLUES SCALE (with bends)
 0:38

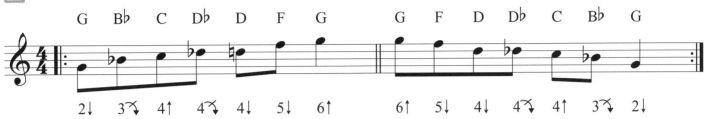

Now let's start working towards playing this scale by leaving a few notes out. This will give us the *bluesy* sound of the 2nd-position scale, which we can do a lot with, while also allowing us to leave out the bends until we're ready. Play the following notes, then repeat. The more you play these notes, the more you'll move yourself closer to playing improvised blues (even without knowing the bends).

SIMPLIFIED G BLUES SCALE (no bends)
 1:10

Now let's turn the quarter notes into eighth notes and double each hole. Breathe from your diaphragm in the low end of your belly and back. These notes all sound pretty good when played against a 12-bar blues (see progression below).

BLUES SCALE EXERCISE
 2:11

The video for this next 12-bar blues progression includes a guitar accompaniment so you can play along using any combination of notes from the G simplified blues scale—in any order and as many times as you'd like—to see and hear what I'm talking about. It's amazing! Once you know where the notes are, it's really hard to play a bad note. However, the more techniques, riffs, exercises, and songs that you learn, the better your solos will start to sound.

12-BAR BLUES
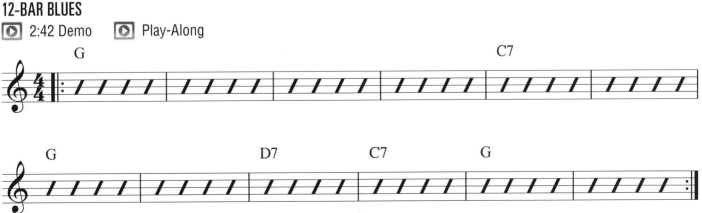 2:42 Demo   Play-Along

NO-BEND CROSS-HARP LICKS

There are literally thousands of bluesy riffs and phrases based on the "no-bend" simplified blues scale. For the next couple of pages, we're going to focus on helping you become proficient at playing in 2nd position. To accomplish this goal, we'll use licks, tunes, and exercises. All aboard! Here we go!

The first lick is a blues **turnaround** lick, which is a musical phrase played in the last few bars of a blues song that helps to "turn" the progression "around" for the repeat back to the beginning of the form. Turnarounds can also be used as an intro to a song. Be sure to listen to Sonny Boy Williamson (aka Rice Miller), who used to play a lot of turnarounds of this type with added hand tremolo.

LICK 1

This next lick is in the spirit of the late, great Sonny Terry. It can be played over the I chord in a 12-bar blues.

LICK 2

The third no-bend blues lick is a generic shuffle pattern that harpists use to accompany a 12-bar shuffle or boogie type of progression (see the next page for more about these patterns). If you play the repeats, this equals four total measures. In a 12-bar blues, this pattern could be played over eight of the 12 standard bars, making this a great lick to know. These phrases are played in eighth notes, so count "1 and 2 and 3 and 4 and."

LICK 3

The last example is another triplet-based lick that can be played over almost any chord change in a 12-bar progression.

LICK 4

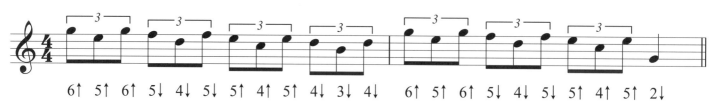

30

BOOGIE AND SHUFFLE BLUES PATTERNS

The following is a basic 12-bar boogie in G that doesn't use bends. This is a must-know pattern for those of us who endeavor to play blues harp! Every piece of this basic boogie could potentially become the basis for solos, riffs, and accompaniment at jam sessions. In addition to the practical nature of recycling these phrases, the use of double tonguing to play these patterns is imperative (see page 15 for a review).

THE SHUFFLE FEEL

Many styles of music, especially blues and jazz, use a type of rhythm called the **shuffle feel** (or **swing feel**), in which eighth notes are played unevenly. Instead of two eighth notes dividing one beat into two equal parts, the beat is divided into *three* parts like a triplet. The first eighth note lasts as long as the first two notes of a triplet tied together, resulting in a "long-short" rhythm feel.

In standard music notation, eighth notes are still shown the same way as usual, but the start of the song will include some type of indication that tells you to shuffle the eighths, like "Shuffle feel," as seen in the next example. This is a very common type of rhythm that you've certainly heard many times throughout popular music. Watch and listen to the video performance of the next example to hear it in action.

NO-BEND BOOGIE

0:40

Shuffle feel

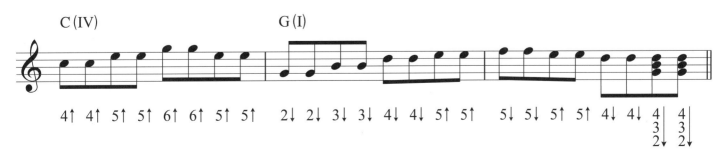

CROSS-HARP AGILITY EXERCISES

TRIPLETS

Earlier in the book, you learned that triplets are three-note groupings, typically dividing one beat into three notes. Triplets appear in every genre of music and in every time signature; they are used extensively in blues, jazz, and rock soloing. Here's how they appear in a 4/4 measure in Ex. 1, and in conjunction with other notes in Ex. 2:

Ex. 1   **Ex. 2**

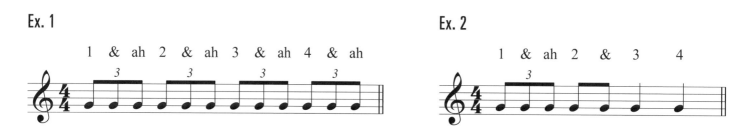

The first exercise below is a bluesy triplet scale run (minus the bends). This is a sweet little exercise that you should play a couple times a week to improve your rhythm, speed, and soloing chops.

TRIPLET EXERCISE 1

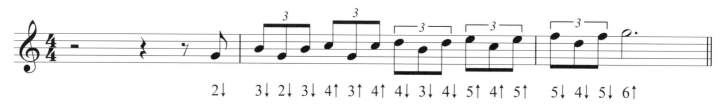

The next exercise shows you how powerful a simple repeating triplet can be, making this an essential idea in a typical 12-bar blues solo.

TRIPLET EXERCISE 2

The third triplet exercise combines two repeating triplet phrases into one very effective lick. Play these slowly at first, and then build up speed over a few weeks of practice. Go back to page 29 and try playing these over the 12-Bar Blues example to hear how great they sound with another instrument.

TRIPLET EXERCISE 3

PLAYING OCTAVES

An **octave** is the distance between two notes with the same letter name. For instance, the 4-hole blow and the 7-hole blow are both C—the same note but in different octaves; one is higher in register than the other. Two notes that are an octave apart always sound similar. By combining them both together, their frequency doubles—a very cool effect that harp players use to fatten up their sound. Remember the old adage, "two heads are better than one"? Well, the same holds true for notes on the harmonica—two notes are better than one!

Looking at the image below, notice the circles (lips) around holes 1 through 4. Now notice how holes 2 and 3 are blacked out; this represents the tip of the tongue pressing forward onto holes 2 and 3, while allowing 1 and 4 to be blown or drawn. Octaves require the tip of the tongue to block off unintended holes; this is what allows us to play an octave without getting all the extra notes. Please note that there are many more octaves and other note combinations available on the harmonica. This lesson is a starting point for the beginning student to use as a springboard into more advanced tongue-blocking studies later on.

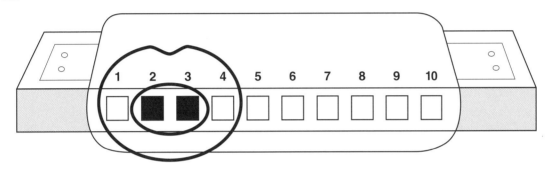

Let's begin by playing the major scale with as many octaves as we can. Note that we don't have an available octave on holes 5, 6, and 7 draw, so we'll just play the single-note draws. Play this example once, and then go back and play it several dozen times until using the tip of your tongue feels normal.

MAJOR SCALE WITH OCTAVES
 1:58

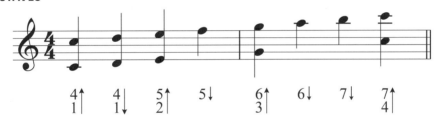

A spiritual dating back to the American Civil War, "Michael Row Your Boat Ashore"—recorded by everyone from the Smothers Brothers to Harry Belafonte and the Weavers—has enjoyed many appearances on the hit parade. Originally passed via oral tradition in African-American communities like Johns Island and St. Helena Island, this memorable melody is the perfect piece to practice playing octaves, as well as hand tremolo. To begin, review the basic melody on page 8, and then come back and try it using octaves.

MICHAEL ROW YOUR BOAT ASHORE (Octaves)
 3:00

The next exercise is designed to help you become more proficient at playing octaves around the middle register. Go slow, and then try to build up speed. This will train you to be able to play songs that are both fast and slow. Remember, use the tip of your tongue to block out the two holes that fall between the two notes you intend to play.

ZIG-ZAG OCTAVE EXERCISE

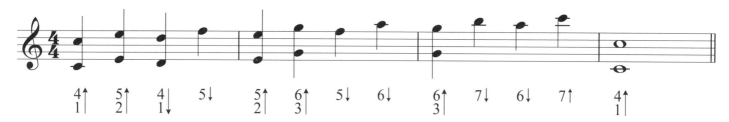

USING OCTAVES IN BLUES

Big Walter Horton (1921–1981) was one of the all-time great Chicago blues harp players. Like Little Walter, his innovative use of amplification with the harmonica helped solidify the instrument as a staple in blues bands from Memphis to Chicago. His classic recorded instrumentals "The Honeydripper," "Big Walter's Boogie," "Easy," and "Have a Good Time" are some of the finest examples of incredible tone, style, taste, and *the use of octaves* in blues harp history.

Blues lyricist and Chess Records talent scout Willie Dixon once said, "Big Walter Horton was, far and away, the best harmonica player in the world!" Coming from a man who played with some of the best, that's quite a compliment. See my top ten blues harp records on the next page and listen for yourself!

The 12-bar blues below illustrates how to take a number of licks and riffs and combine them into one solo. The use of repeating octave riffs, single notes, hand tremolo, and triplets all make for a dynamic example of classic blues harp flavor!

PICKUPS

Did you notice the extra short measure at the beginning of "Blowing the Blues Like Big Walter"? The opening triplet starts *before* the first measure, on beat 4. This is called a **pickup**, which appears often in music. Count "1, 2, 3," and then play the triplet on beat 4 to begin the solo.

BLOWING THE BLUES LIKE BIG WALTER

0:09

How good you become playing the blues on the harmonica has a lot to do with how much time you've spent soaking up licks from the real harp masters! Everybody loves top 10 lists, so here's one to guide you—this is the real harmonica mojo!

Lil' Rev's Picks: The Top Ten Best Blues-Harp Records of All Time

1. *Hoodoo Man Blues* – Junior Wells' Chicago Blues Band, Delmark Records, 1965

2. *Big Walter Horton with Carey Bell* – Big Walter Horton, Alligator Records, 1972

3. *Down and Out Blues* – Sonny Boy Williamson, Checker Records, 1959

4. *Stand Back! Here Comes Charley Musselwhite's South Side Band* – Charlie Musselwhite, Vanguard Records, 1967

5. *His Best: The Chess 50th Anniversary Collection* – Little Walter, Chess Records, 1997

6. *Blowin' Like Hell* – William Clarke, Alligator Records, 1990

7. *High Compression* – James Cotton, Alligator Records, 1984

8. *Sonny Terry and Brownie McGhee at Sugar Hill* – Sonny Terry & Brownie McGhee, Fantasy Records, 1961

9. *Brownie McGhee and Sonny Terry Sing* – Sonny Terry & Brownie McGhee, Smithsonian/Folkways, 1958

10. *Dog Days of August* – Cephas & Wiggins, Flying Fish Records, 1984

TEN TIPS FOR GREAT HARP TONE ▶

What does great harp tone sound like and how does one achieve it? I would define great harp tone as a clear, strong sound that is complimented by a player's ability to use a proper lip and jaw **embouchure** (how you apply your lips and mouth to an instrument), as well as hand, throat, and diaphragmatic **vibrato**. Vibrato is similar to tremolo but focuses more on wavering the *pitch* than the volume.

When it comes to the harmonica, sound *pressure* is really the key to achieving the kind of pleasing tonal frequencies that resonate from schooled harp players. This means knowing how to drop, or lower, your jaw over any harp hole to achieve a clear, acoustic sound. If you are as little as 1/16 of an inch off, your jaw will be too narrow—i.e., your teeth too far forward—and your tone will immediately change, often sounding "clucky," sloppy, breathy, or choked.

In blues harp playing, the 2-hole draw is *the* most important hole. It is "home base," and you need to be able to nail that hole cleanly, as well as with vibrato. How you open your mouth, shape your jaw, and form an embouchure over the top and bottom of the harp is key to achieving this goal (see Tips below).

As my friend, tone-master, and Milwaukee guitar maven Jim "High Noon" Eannelli once told me, "You can't force-feed good tone." Tone is something that you strive towards; it's a combination of all the practice you've done and the players you've watched, listened to, and learned from. More importantly, great tone doesn't come in an old, beat-up Masco Tube PA or the JT-30 Astatic crystal microphone that you scored on eBay; it starts with you—the player, not the equipment!

Tip 1: Learn how to hold the harmonica so that you can create an "airtight" sound chamber. By cupping both hands around the harp, you'll gain full control of how the sound will be directed once it's played. (The ultimate master of this is Phil Wiggins of Cephas & Wiggins.)

Tip 2: Listen to many recordings of legendary harp players to hear what good tone sounds like. Likewise, watch harp players' throats and bellies to identify the body language of proper technique. (Listen to Big Walter, Sonny Boy Williamson, William Clarke, and Paul Butterfield.)

Tip 3: Watch the video (2:31) and practice my throat vibrato exercise daily.

Tip 4: Watch the video (4:00) and practice my diaphragmatic exercise daily.

Tip 5: Know the difference between using a narrow embouchure and a wide embouchure. (Often, this is an essential distinction between playing in 1st or 2nd position.)

Tip 6: Don't just practice good tonal techniques on the draw notes, practice them on the blow notes as well.

Tip 7: Listen for the spots in a song or melody where the note values are longer. Soon you'll learn how to fill in the holes with great tone and the techniques that support it.

Tip 8: Find a respected local harmonica teacher or online source with whom you can dig deeper into the subject of great harp tone.

Tip 9: Starting with the simplified blues scale, say "Ooooo" on each hole, both draw and blow.

Tip 10: Remember—feeling, tone, and technique come first! Once you have these, *then* it's time to explore and master the use of amplifiers, effects, and microphones.

BENDING NOTES ▶️

Most seasoned harp players will tell you that learning to bend notes was the single biggest game-changer on their journey towards achieving harmonica nirvana. Now it's your turn to work towards that goal.

GETTING STARTED

Before we dig in deep, here are a few important things to consider:

- Bending is all about using the right amount of airflow.
- The air pressure that you apply to each hole determines how the reeds vibrate and, likewise, determines the pitch.
- Holes 1–6 are draw bends. Holes 7–10 are blow bends.
- This book focuses on the most commonly used bends—the draw bends on holes 1–6.

To begin bending, start by breathing in and saying the following words…

1. **Wee-Ooo:** As you say "wee-ooo," notice that your lower jaw drops down and your tongue tucks into the soft palate, just in front of your lower front teeth. The tongue is slightly hunched in the back. Repeat "wee-ooo" a couple dozen times, while breathing in and breathing out.

2. **Oy-You:** Now, repeat the same as above, but this time say "oy-you" while breathing in.

These phrases, and others like them, will help shape your jaw, mouth, and lips into the proper position that is needed to play bends.

3. Pick up your harmonica and find the 2-hole draw note. Breathe in while trying to say "wee-ooo." Can you hear the pitch change at all? If not, try increasing the amount of air you draw in as you say "wee-ooo." Now can you hear a change?

4. Next, find hole 1, and draw in while saying "oy-you." Try to increase the amount of air you are taking in gradually as you say "oy-you." Hole 1 is the easiest hole to learn how to bend on. I am betting that you're having much success! If so, keep going, because each hole requires a unique adjustment of the jaw, mouth, lips, and breath in order to bend a note.

This diagram shows how many different bent notes are available from each draw hole in the lower and middle registers of the harmonica.

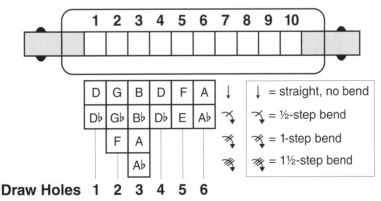

Draw Holes 1 2 3 4 5 6

ACCIDENTALS

Now that you have started bending notes, you are able to produce new pitches that are not normally possible on a diatonic harmonica—pitches that are *in between* the natural notes of the musical alphabet. In standard notation, we use **sharps** (♯) and **flats** (♭) to raise or lower the natural notes. For instance, the 1-hole draw bend produces a D♭ ("D flat"), which is a half step below the natural D. We are bending the D *down* to D♭. Likewise, a sharp raises a natural note by a half step. D♯ would be a half step *higher* than D. If a note changes back to its natural state within the same measure or the following one, we add a **natural** (♮) symbol to the note. Collectively, these notation symbols are known as **accidentals**.

HOLES 1–3

We'll begin learning to bend notes with the 1-hole draw. Gently draw in on the 1-hole and you'll get a D note. Now draw in and say "wee-ooo," while gradually increasing the amount of air, until you hear the note begin to flatten to D♭. Let's practice doing this repetitively.

1-HOLE DRAW BENDS

 2:28

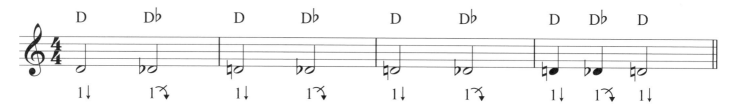

The 2-hole draw can produce two or more bent notes: a half-step bend down to G♭ and a whole-step bend down to F. If we add the straight, 2-hole draw G note, that's three notes total we're producing on the 2-hole draw.

2-HOLE DRAW BENDS

 3:59

There are four distinct notes that can be played when drawing on the 3-hole, starting with the no-bend B note, followed by B♭, A, and A♭. This means there are three bent notes to master on the third hole, in addition to the 3-hole regular draw note, which is a B note.

3-HOLE DRAW BENDS

 4:25

Here's a tune we played earlier in the book in 1st position. Let's try it in 2nd position now, using a whole-step bend on the 3-hole to play the A notes.

GOODNIGHT LADIES (2nd Position)

 4:38

B	G	D	G		B	G	A	A		B	G	C	C		C	B	B	A	A	G
3↓	2↓	1↓	2↓		3↓	2↓	3↘	3↘		3↓	2↓	4↑	4↑		4↑	3↓	3↓	3↘	3↘	2↓

This delightfully catchy little melody has been around forever. Take a moment to watch the video, then give it a shot! There's one whole-step bend on the 3-hole draw (A) that appears in both the A and B sections of this tune.

LI'L LIZA JANE

 4:53

2ND POSITION TIPS

Just as you've already done with 1st position, for 2nd position, start with a variety of simple folk songs and timeless melodies that are easy to master. Once you've learned a couple dozen of the classics, then you'll be ready for rock, pop, blues, country, jazz, hip-hop, and more!

Here's a really simple tune that's great for perfecting your 3-hole draw bends. Like "Li'l Liza Jane," this has a whole-step draw bend that produces an A note.

LONDON BRIDGE IS FALLING DOWN

5:17

Lon - don	Bridge	is	fall - ing	down,	fall - ing	down,	fall - ing	down.
4↓ 5↑	4↓	4↑	3↓ 4↑	4↓	3↘ 3↓	4↑	3↓ 4↑	4↓

Lon - don	Bridge	is	fall - ing	down,	my	fair	la - dy.
4↓ 5↑	4↓	4↑	3↓ 4↑	4↓	3↘	4↓	3↓ 2↓

This all-time classic blues riff contains a killer half-step 3-hole bend to the bluesy B♭:

CLASSIC CHICAGO BLUES RIFF

5:32

(repeat as desired)

$\|:$ G   C   B♭   G   :$\|$

2↓   4↑   3↘   2↓   4↓   4↓   4↓   4↓
                                            3↓   3↓   3↓   3↓
                                            2↓   2↓   2↓   2↓

HOLES 4–6

Remember, you can always start with "wee-ooo" to reset your sense of how the jaw, mouth, and lips should be positioned when learning to bend. Also, please remember that some holes are harder to bend than others, so you'll need to be patient with yourself as you learn to navigate bending. There are two notes available on the 4-hole draw. One is the straight D note, and the other is a half-step bend down to D♭.

4-HOLE DRAW BENDS

0:04

There are two draw notes on hole 5: a no-bend F note, and a half-step bend down to E.

5-HOLE DRAW BENDS

0:28

Six-hole draw is an A note. There is also a half-step bend down to A♭. You're doing a great job practicing these bends! Remember, the key is repetition!

6-HOLE DRAW BENDS

1:22

THE HEADSHAKE

In the following blues example, you'll find a new technique in the last measure known as "the headshake," or **trill**. Watch me demonstrate this in the video. Essentially, I'm drawing in on holes 4 and 5 while shaking my head side to side. This creates a warbling effect that is a staple in every blues harp player's grab bag. This type of warble can be done with drawing or blowing.

CRAZY MIXED-UP BENT-NOTE BLUES

1:54

STANDARD BLUES LICKS

What follows are six stock blues harp licks—some with bends and some without. Most of these licks will be helpful as you continue to try and master draw bends.

The first is a classic chordal train lick, followed by a bluesy tag ending lick.

LICK 1

LICK 2

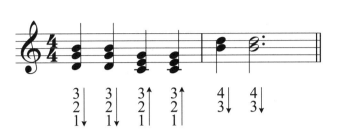

Here is a Sonny Boy Williamson-style triplet lick. Watch for the half-step bend on the 4-hole.

LICK 3

Lick 4 is a 1950s doo-wop triplet riff. Say "do-do-do" for each triplet.

LICK 4

Check out this cool Howlin' Wolf-style riff:

LICK 5

And here's a more challenging triplet idea:

LICK 6

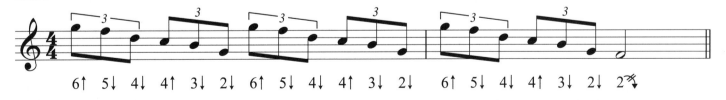

BENDING MONSTERS

If you'd like to hear some of the greatest bending masters, I recommend seeking out the recorded work and videos of Junior Wells, Snooky Pryor, James Cotton, Jimmy Reed, John Popper, Steve Cohen, Jim Liban, Rod Piazza, Kim Wilson, Huey Lewis, Charlie McCoy, Brendan Power, Annie Raines, and Joe Filisko to name a few.

TWO BENDING HACKS

Let's be honest… bending notes on the blues harp doesn't always come easy. Trust me, you're not alone. All of us who've achieved some level of proficiency have initially felt the same frustration that you may be feeling right now. Patience and persistence are the key to beating those mean, old bent-note blues. Below are two bending hacks to help!

The Tilt

"The tilt" is a cheater technique that will help you hear how a bent note can, and should, sound. It is not a tool that you can use to play a song or a riff, but it will help you hear the difference between a straight note and a bent note. Below are the instructions on how to do the tilt.

1. Hold the harmonica in your left hand. Draw in on hole 1.

2. Say "oy-you" while breathing in.

3. As you get to the word "you," tilt the harmonica upwards gradually.

4. If you still can't hear a change in pitch, then try it again. But this time, inhale *much harder* on the word "you." This will affect the reeds in a manner that makes it easier for them to bend. Try this a few times until you can hear the change in pitch. Remember that bending is all about learning to control the amount of air that is directed towards those little brass reeds.

5. Now, try this same technique on holes 2–6, and each time, tilt the harmonica upwards on the word "you" while increasing the air flow as well.

The Hand-Wah Effect

The "hand-wah" effect is based off of the hand tremolo technique that you learned earlier in the book. Each time the hand opens, it gently distorts the pitch. When the pitch isn't allowed to flow freely out of the harmonica, it can create the illusion of a bent note, especially if you try to make the wah sound while doing it. It's sometimes called a "fake bend." Here are the specific instructions on how to do the wah effect.

1. Hold the harmonica in your left hand.

2. Wrap your right hand around the top of your left hand, allowing the right-hand thumb to rest gently underneath the harp.

3. Play the C major scale, and with each note, try to say "wah" while simultaneously opening the right hand on each "wah." This will create a bluesy, bent note-like effect.

4↑ 4↓ 5↑ 5↓ 6↑ 6↓ 7↓ 7↑

4. Go back and play the C major scale again, this time saying "wah-wah" on each hole.

5. Now, try this with the simplified blues scale that you learned on page 29. Say "wah" on each hole while opening up your hand to shape the sound as it comes out.

2↓ 3↓ 4↑ 4↓ 5↓ 6↑

BENDING THE BLUES

SONGS WITH BENDS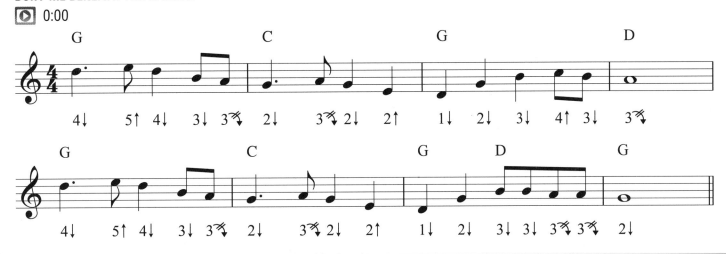

"Bury Me Beneath the Willow" dates back to the late 1800s. I've arranged this old folk tune in 2nd position with a bluesy flavor, using the 3-hole, whole-step draw bend to play the A notes. This piece will show you how the blues approach can be used in a country-flavored piece.

BURY ME BENEATH THE WILLOW
0:00

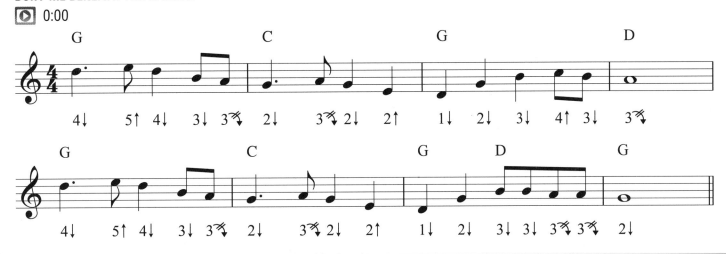

ENHARMONICS

In the next song, notice that the 4-hole draw bend is written as a C# instead of a D♭. That's because D♭ and C# are the same note! These notes are called **enharmonics**, which are, essentially, a different way to represent the same note. Here are the enharmonics for the four flatted notes you can draw bend:

D♭ = C#   G♭ = F#   B♭ = A#   A♭ = G#

Jed Davenport was a famous jug-band blues musician from Memphis whose expressive harmonica playing stands as some of the era's finest. There are three different bends to hit on this one! While most blues compositions are in 4/4 time, "Jed Davenport's Blues" gives us a nice opportunity to practice our chops in waltz time, or 3/4, making this piece a refreshing twist in the blues dance. Remember to count "1-2-3, 1-2-3."

JED DAVENPORT'S BLUES
0:18

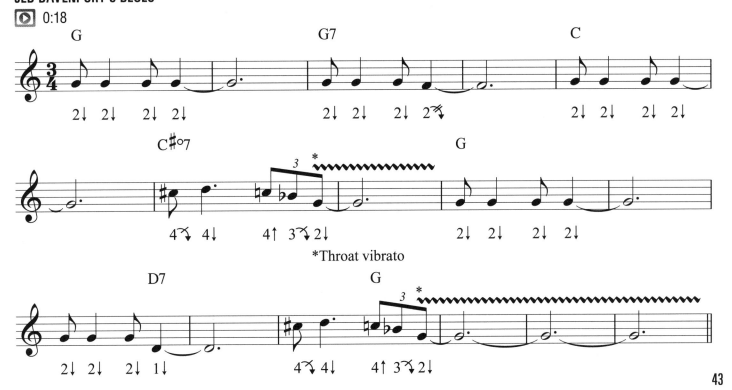

*Throat vibrato

EXERCISES AND SONGS

Let's begin with an exercise that will train you to hit a bent note, and then quickly shift to a regular pitch. "The Fastest Draw in the Land" has you bending each hole in this way, from hole 6 to hole 1. Getting this technique down has been a real game-changer for a lot of my students. Be sure to give this a lot of repetition!

THE FASTEST DRAW IN THE LAND
 0:00

"(Hang Down Your Head) Tom Dooley," also known as "Tom Dula's Blues," is an old folk song that found its way into the hands of song catchers in the deep South, passed along by banjo players like Frank Proffitt to others like Doc Watson and the Kingston Trio—each making their own inimitable versions. Perhaps you'll do the same! Watch the 3-hole whole-step bends. Play each hole cleanly and clearly!

(HANG DOWN YOUR HEAD) TOM DOOLEY
 0:11

This is a great low-end workout in 3/4 time. "Rye Whiskey," also known as "The Drunkard's Hiccups," is said to have come to America via the Scottish/Irish influence. There is a quarter-note pickup at the start (on beat 3) and one whole-step bend to A at the end.

RYE WHISKEY
 0:26

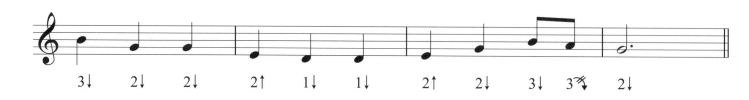

"Handsome Molly" is a traditional piece, arranged on the next page to provide more practice with low-end bends. This song first appeared in the Cecil Sharp Collection of 1918, and has since been recorded by Mick Jagger, Bob Dylan, and the Stanley Brothers, to name a few.

The 3-hole bends give the tune a blues flavor that is right at home with many folk, country, and bluegrass favorites. The real lesson here is to be able to hit two consecutive bends in a row, as found in measure 3. This catchy little arrangement can be played over the verse as well as the chorus.

Verse

I wish I was in London, or some other seaport town;

I set my foot on a steamboat, and sail the ocean 'round.

Chorus

Sailing 'round the ocean, sailing 'round the sea,

Think of handsome Molly, wherever she may be.

HANDSOME MOLLY

 0:42

TALKING HARMONICA

 1:00

The harmonica has always been a staple in every era of recorded sound. None have been more interesting than the wealth of "talking blues" that were recorded in the mid-1920s through the '50s by artists like DeFord Bailey, Sonny Terry, Salty Holmes, Lonnie Glosson, and Wayne Raney. "I want my momma" and "I want a little drink of water" were common, harp-spoken themes. The reason for the rise in this type of impressive showpiece is simple—the harmonica is one of the most expressive and emotive instruments.

The harmonica can laugh, cry, cackle, chirp, bark, buzz, and imitate almost anything that the mind can conceive. Perhaps that's why the harmonica has always been a favorite of Hollywood, where its ability to create ambience, suspense, sadness, mystery, or joy makes it the instrument of choice for moviemakers the world over.

Here's how to play a short-but-sweet, generic rendition of the talking blues, saying "I want my momma."

1. Draw in on the 3-hole to say the word "I."

2. Draw in on a 3-hole whole-step bend to say the word "want."

3. Draw in on the 2-hole (G note, no bend) to say the word "my."

4. Draw in two times in a row on a 3-hole whole-step bend to say "momma."

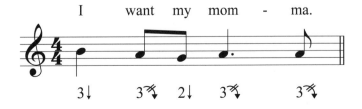

Repeat this phrase one more time, and then combine it with the "No-Bend Boogie" on page 31 to create a real showstopper!

PLAYING IN MINOR KEYS— 3RD POSITION

As you begin to build a repertoire of songs to play on the harmonica, soon you'll discover that playing in minor keys requires a different approach than the major-scale-based music that we've started with. "Double-cross" or **3rd position** is what harp players use to play in minor keys.

To play in 3rd position, we'll use all of the notes in the C major scale, except we'll shift our root note from C to the 2nd degree of the C major scale, which is D (C-**D**-E-F-G-A-B-C). So, if we start on the 4-hole draw (D) and continue up to the 8-hole draw, which is also a D note, we'll have the following notes: D-E-F-G-A-B-C-D. On a C harp, this scale puts us in D minor. This isn't the *true* minor scale, but a variation of it known as the **Dorian mode**, or the Dorian scale.

DORIAN MODE
 0:32

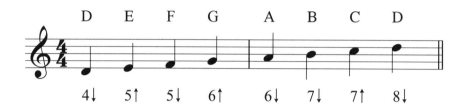

Now let's play the old "double or nothing" game. Once you get good at this one, then triple every hole!

DOUBLE DORIAN
 0:46

If you're willing to utilize your newly acquired low-end bending skills, we can also play the 3rd-position scale in the lower octave by using two whole-step bends—including one on the 2-hole (F) and one on the 3-hole (A). This is another version of the scale that is worth memorizing.

DORIAN MODE (with bends)

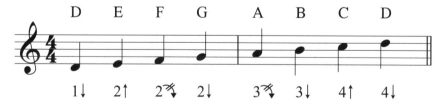

If you enjoyed learning how to sweeten up the sound of your harp using octaves (pages 33–35), you can easily apply these same skills when playing in 3rd position. Here's D Dorian played with octaves.

DORIAN MODE (Octaves)

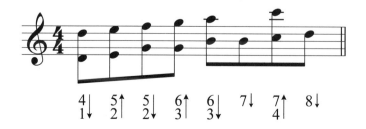

SONGS IN MINOR KEYS

Below is a handy reference chart that shows the different harps you would need in order to play in different minor keys. The scale remains the same, but the keys will change, so it's good to own a variety of harps in different keys so you can be flexible. For example, C, D, F, G, A, and B♭ would be the best six harps to own to be prepared to play in a bunch of different keys.

The best way to remember which harmonica to use for any given minor key is to ask your fellow musician friends what key the song is in. If they say "A minor," grab your G harp; if they say "D minor," grab your C harp; if they say "E minor," grab your D harp… etc. Just think one step back from the song's key and that's the fastest way to figure out which harp to grab!

Key of Song	Key of Harp Played in 3rd Position
Am	G
Bm	A
Cm	B♭
Dm	C
Em	D
Fm	E♭
Gm	F

Here are a couple of songs in D minor to get you started playing melodies in 3rd position. We'll begin with "Sinner Man," a timeless spiritual.

SINNER MAN

 0:00

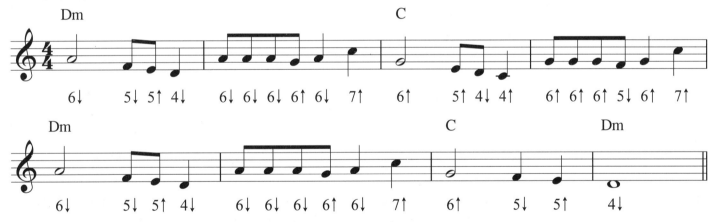

The following song is an Appalachian classic called "Cluck Old Hen," which I played earlier in the book (page 24) with a hurricane lamp shade! This is a Dorian version in 3rd position.

CLUCK OLD HEN

My	old	hen's	a	good	old	hen,		she	lays	eggs	for	the	rail - road	men.
6↓	8↓	7↑	8↓	6↓	8↓	7↑		6↓	8↓	7↑	8↓	7↑	6↓6↑	5↓	4↓

Some-times	one,		some-times	two,		some-times	e-nough for	the	whole	darn	crew!
6↓	8↓	7↑	6↓	8↓	7↑	6↓	8↓ 8↓ 7↑ 8↓	7↑	6↓6↑	5↓	4↓

Cluck	old	hen,	cluck	and	sing,		ain't	laid	an	egg	since	way	last	spring.
4↓	4↓	5↓	4↓	4↓	4↑		4↓	4↓	4↓	5↓	6↑	6↓6↑	5↓	4↓

Cluck	old	hen,	cluck	and	squall,		ain't	laid	an	egg	since	way	last	fall.
4↓	4↓	5↓	4↓	4↓	4↑		4↓	4↓	4↓	5↓	6↑	6↓6↑	5↓	4↓

"Hinei Mah Tov" is a Hebrew folk tune with lyrics derived from Psalm 133:1. Often sung in a round, it is a beautiful melody that sounds fabulous in 3rd position. The time signature for this is 3/4, so remember to count each measure "1, 2, 3." Note that each part is repeated. This is called an "AABB" song format.

HINEI MAH TOV

▶ 0:19

"Zum Gali Gali" is another really fun piece to play in 3rd position. Like "Hinei Mah Tov," this melody is often sung as a round and is a perennial camp favorite. There's a 3-hole whole-step draw bend in the A section that you've been training for, so give it your best shot!

ZUM GALI GALI

▶ 0:53

*Throat vibrato

The last 3rd-position melody we'll work on is a toe-tapping, two-chord sea shanty. Whenever you encounter a lot of draw notes in a row, you'll need to use double tonguing (see page 15). This is accomplished by allowing the tongue to flutter up and down while breathing in. To do this with the rhythm of "The Drunken Sailor" below, say "dit dit-dit, dit dit-dit" as you draw in on hole 6. You'll feel your tongue moving up and down properly; this will allow you to play many consecutive draw notes in rapid succession.

THE DRUNKEN SAILOR